Seasons and Reasons

Poems and Prayers

Gwendoline Sissons

ISBN:9798332048197

Independently published

All rights reserved. No part of this publication may be reproduced, stored in a retrieval system, or transmitted in any form or by any means, electronic, mechanical, photocopying, recording or otherwise, without the prior permission of the author.

All artwork @Bellesaqua

Contents

Introduction..1

Hello Spring..4
Wonderful Spring...5
Spring beautiful Spring...7
The Work of His hands..9

Hello Summer..12
Summer Glory...13
A perfect Summer day..15
Beauty all around us..17

Hello Autumn..20
Awesome Autumn...21

Hello Winter..24
Winter nears..25

Christmas..28
Christmas is...29
The sparkle of Christmas..31
Let's celebrate!..33

Ever Constant...35

Praises to the Lord...38
Lord of all, we praise You..39
The Lord's goodness..41
Praise for the Lord..43
A prayer of praise...45
Thank You prayer...47
We give thanks...49
Thank You Lord...51

Stillness..54
In the stillness..55
Rain and stillness...57
Precious stillness..59
Reflection time/prayer/praise..61

Introduction (to the book)

Dear reader,

The poems and prayers in this book were written over a span of three years, after finding my way back to my Christian faith in 2018.

The first poem which I wrote back in April 2021 and called "Ever Constant" (page 35) was a true account of the conflicting weather conditions at that time. Since writing "Ever Constant" I have been very inspired to write more poetry as well as prayers to express my heartfelt love and gratitude for our wonderful creator God and for His precious Son, Jesus.

I have always been in awe of the different seasons, each one bringing its own uniqueness, beauty and purpose for the Earth and for life itself. Several seasonal poems and prayers are therefore included in this book.

What a magnificent world our God has provided to us! As we look all around us, we can see the wonders of His creation and countless miracles.

Such was the inspiration for most of my poetry and prayers and I cannot thank and praise our God enough for all that He does and gives. There are so many reasons to glorify our heavenly Father who loves us unconditionally.

Introduction (to the book) continued.

I have also included poems and prayers which reflect upon precious solitary and quiet moments, a time to be still and to know and acknowledge that He is God.

It is an absolute blessing for me to have this book published and to share my poems and prayers with you.

I pray that some of the poetry and prayers will bless you too and bring you closer to our most gracious and generous God. A few pages are available at the end of the book for your own reflections.

All praise and glory to our wonderful, loving, comforting, almighty, creator God.

In Jesus name…Amen

A few extra words;
With my heartfelt thanks to my dearest friend Isabelle for letting me use her beautiful, God inspired artwork to accompany each poem and prayer.

Gwen

"The heavens declare the glory of God; the skies proclaim the work of His hands.
Psalm 19:1 - NIV

Hello Spring

To everything there is a season,
A time for every purpose under heaven:
Ecclesiastes 3: 1 - NKJV

Wonderful Spring

Wonderful Spring

The wonderful season of Spring is now here,
a fresh beginning, new life starts to appear.

As we look around us, we see beauty unfold,
blankets of bright and beautiful flowers, such a sight to behold.

New green shoots and leaves are Spring declaring,
happy and tuneful birds are busy preparing.

Father, we thank You for this glorious Spring season and
for all the joy and hope that it does bring,

We praise and adore You for all of your magnificent creation,
as it truly makes our grateful hearts sing.

Spring beautiful Spring

Spring, beautiful Spring.

Spring, beautiful Spring, it's such a delight,
Birds are happily nesting and chirping away,
Colourful tulips, bluebells and others in sight,
Rays of sunshine break through each day.

Spring, beautiful Spring, all is fresh and new,
A feeling of joy and hope for the days ahead,
Green is in abundance and skies are vivid blue,
New shoots wait proudly in their garden bed.

Spring, beautiful Spring, Lord we are in awe,
Another new season, a miracle within creation,
We are so full of praise and will be evermore,
All glory to You, with thanks and adoration.

The work of His hands

The work of His hands

We see You in the skies Lord, in every shining star,

In the sun and in the moon, Your presence is never far.

We see You in the oceans Lord, with each and every drift,
In coastal views and sunsets, everything is such a gift.

We see You in the flowers Lord, in every shape and kind,
In colourful foliage, trees and plants, You are never far from mind.

We see You in the mountains Lord, in each and every crest,
In green valleys and still rivers, we are truly blessed.

We see You in butterflies and birds Lord, as they soar freely towards the skies,
In every creature great and small, all a vision to our eyes.

We see You everywhere Lord, as we gaze around us in praise and with love,
In the wonder of all that we have been given from our Heavenly Father above.

Hello Summer

From the rising of the sun to its going down
The Lord's name *is* to be praised.
Psalm 113:3 - NKJV

Summer glory

Summer glory

Dear Lord,

Thank You for this new summer season,
For the warmth and golden, sunshine rays.
As we look around us, there is every reason,
To lift up our hands to You in glory and praise.

Thank You for colourful birds and busy bees,
For the tuneful songs and honey each bring.
As we look around at the majestic trees,
A sense of wonderment and joy flows within.

Thank You for beautiful flowers, such an array,
For every design and delicate scent.
As we look up to the sky on this perfect day,
A feeling of peace makes our hearts content.

Thank You for this glorious summer season,
For the warmth and golden, sunshine rays.
As we look around us, there is every reason,
To lift up our hearts to You in endless praise.

Amen

A perfect Summer day

A perfect summer day

How should I describe my perfect summer day?
With so many words to choose from in a varying way?

Perhaps a day completely free from worry or fear?
Or afternoon tea in the garden with a person most dear?

Maybe listening to the soothing purring from a very contented cat?
While unwinding in an armchair, what could better that?

Or relaxing on a secluded beach and enjoying the warm sea breeze?
Listening to the melodic songs from garden birds, perched way up high on trees?

Whatever I decide could be a perfect day for me,
May the Lord bring me as much happiness as today did, I will have to wait and see.

Beauty all around us

Beauty all around us

Our world is so beautiful, even words cannot convey,
The splendour that surrounds us, each and every day.

Forests of emerald green and colourful flowers on show,
Butterflies floating and birds soaring, freely in full flow.

The warmth of the sun, a silvery moon, countless stars above,
Crystal blue waters and golden beaches, all created for us
with love.

Sunrises and sunsets, the uniqueness of all the seasons,
Father, we lift up our hearts in praise and we thank You for so
many reasons..

Hello Autumn

... A time to plant and a time to harvest.
Ecclesiastes 3:2 - NLT

Awesome Autumn

Awesome Autumn

Dear Father,

Thank You for this new Autumn season, it's such a wonderful sight to behold,

To be surrounded by a beautiful and colourful tapestry of green, copper, red and gold.

We are so in awe of all of your magnificent creativity, lovingly designed by You,

We are so deeply blessed and grateful to be part of your splendid creation too.

Thank You for the harvest and bountiful food that this Autumn season will bring.

We cannot thank and praise You enough dear Father, for our world, for life, for everything..

Amen

Hello Winter

You set the boundaries of the earth, and You made both summer and **winter**.

Psalm 74:17 - NLT

Winter nears

Winter nears

Dear Father,

The winter season is fast approaching,
It's revealing itself almost everywhere.

All of nature can sense the change,
As there's a frosty, crispy feel in the air.

Small animals are preparing to hibernate,
Storing their energy for the long sleep ahead.

Winter flowering plants are on standby,
Tucked away discreetly in their sheltered bed.

Traces of silver glisten on branches of trees,
Colourful berries are now boldly on show.

Perhaps in the days or weeks ahead,
All could be covered in pristine white snow.

How wonderful to witness every season,
Each unique in its own special way.

A testament to the miracles of creation,
Lovingly provided by You each and every day.

Amen

Christmas

"For to us a child is born, to us a son is given, and the government will be on his shoulders. And He will be called Wonderful Counsellor, Mighty God, Everlasting Father, Prince of Peace."

Isaiah 9:6 - NIV

Christmas is..

Christmas is

Christmas is the most special time of the year,
To celebrate together, in wonder and cheer.

Christmas is so precious, like silver and gold,
To appreciate its value whether young or old.

Christmas is for giving and a time to share,
To be extra kind to others and to offer care.

Christmas is listening out for angelic voices,
To hear choirs sing carols, so full of rejoices.

Christmas is hope and peace for everyone,
To thank God for the gift of his heavenly Son.

Christmas is full of joy, warmth and light,
To keep the love for Jesus, burning bright.

The sparkle of Christmas

The sparkle of Christmas

Lights in shop windows are sparkling brightly, it's a balmy Christmas Eve night,
Festive decorations are adorned everywhere, it's such a wonderful sight.

Children are getting excited and waiting for the special day,
To unwrap their presents with family and to make time together to play.

Choirs are singing carols, it's such a heavenly sound,
As they spread the good news of baby Jesus to everyone all around...

Let's celebrate !

Let's celebrate !

Let's celebrate this wonderful festive season together,

Let our hearts be filled with hope, peace, love and joy.

Let's give praise and heartfelt thanks to our heavenly Father,

For the birth of Jesus, The Light of the World and the most precious baby boy...

Ever constant

"Jesus Christ the same yesterday, and today, and forever."
Hebrews 13:8 KJV

Ever Constant

The seasons come and the seasons go.
When I woke up on that spring morning,
there was a light covering of snow.

Yet just a couple of weeks before,
it had been the hottest day of the year.
A wonderful reminder that the
summer season was drawing near.

How often the seasons merge together,
seemingly without any rhyme or reason.
Yet our Lord Jesus Christ remains ever constant,
His love and light radiating, whatever the
season.

Praises to the Lord

"Praise the LORD. Give thanks to the LORD, for He is good; His love endures forever."

Psalm 106:1 - NIV

Lord of all, we praise You

Lord of all, we praise You

Gracious Lord, almighty maker of heaven and earth,
Let us praise You with words of adoration,
Let us open and lift up our hearts with joy,
Let our thoughts be ever on You.

Faithful Lord, ever loving and merciful Father,
Let us praise You with endless thanks,
Let us bow down in glory of your name,
Let our voices sing in sweet harmony for You.

Comforting Lord, grace us with your presence,
Let us be warmed by your guiding light,
Let us be embraced by your everlasting arms,
Let our whole being be filled by the wonder of You.

The Lord's goodness

The Lord's Goodness

When life becomes overwhelming and full of despair,
Make precious time with the Lord in silence and in prayer.

When lonely thoughts take over and no one seems to care,
Take comfort in the Lord, knowing that He is always there.

When faced with any worries or burdens that may lie ahead on life's road,
Have trust in the Lord for He will carry the load.

Praise for the Lord

Praise for the Lord

Lord, how we love to sing to You with praise,
To bring glory to You throughout our days.

Lord, how we long to feel Your presence near,
To be comforted and free from stress and fear.

Lord, how we treasure each and every day,
To take time to be still with You as we pray.

Lord, how we take delight for all that You do,
To have our hearts brimming with joy for You.

A prayer of praise

A prayer of praise

Creator God,

Thank You for our beautiful world.

For magnificent coastal views, skies so blue and glorious mountains high.

As we look around us and see your wonderful creativity, our hearts are filled with joy and adoration of You.

At times we can feel low and despairing, like a deep and lonely, dark valley.

But as we look up towards the skies and gaze upon the mountains, we feel a sense of drawing ever closer to You.

Thank You for listening to our prayers and for providing us with comfort, guidance, love and light.

In Jesus' name, we praise and thank You.

Amen

Thank You prayer

Thank You prayer

Dear God,

Thank You for guiding us through each day,
Thank You for supporting us come what may.

Thank You for lighting up the way.
Thank You for forgiving us whenever we stray.

Thank You for accepting us for who we are,
Thank You for protecting us from afar.

Thank You for your endless love and grace,
Thank You for providing peace and space.

Thank You for your compassion and care,
Thank You for listening to our every prayer.

Amen

We give thanks

We give thanks

Merciful Father, we give thanks to You for understanding our weaknesses.

Almighty Father, we give thanks to You for the strength and courage bestowed upon us.

Graceful Father, we give thanks to You for your faithfulness and support.

Loving Father, we give thanks to You for your guidance and unconditional love.

All knowing Father, we give thanks to You for every right path laid out before us.

Amen

Thank You Lord

Thank You Lord

Dear Father,

Thank You for guiding us through life's many challenges.

At times, the paths ahead of us seem so daunting and unpredictable.

But just like a bridge, You pave the way for us and provide all the strength and support that we need to overcome each path with courage and steadfastness.

Thank You for loving us unconditionally and for your endless faithfulness.

In Jesus name, we pray and Thank You.

Amen

Stillness

"Be still, and know that I am God:I will be exalted among the heathen, I will be exalted in the earth."

Psalm 46:10 _ KJV

In the stillness

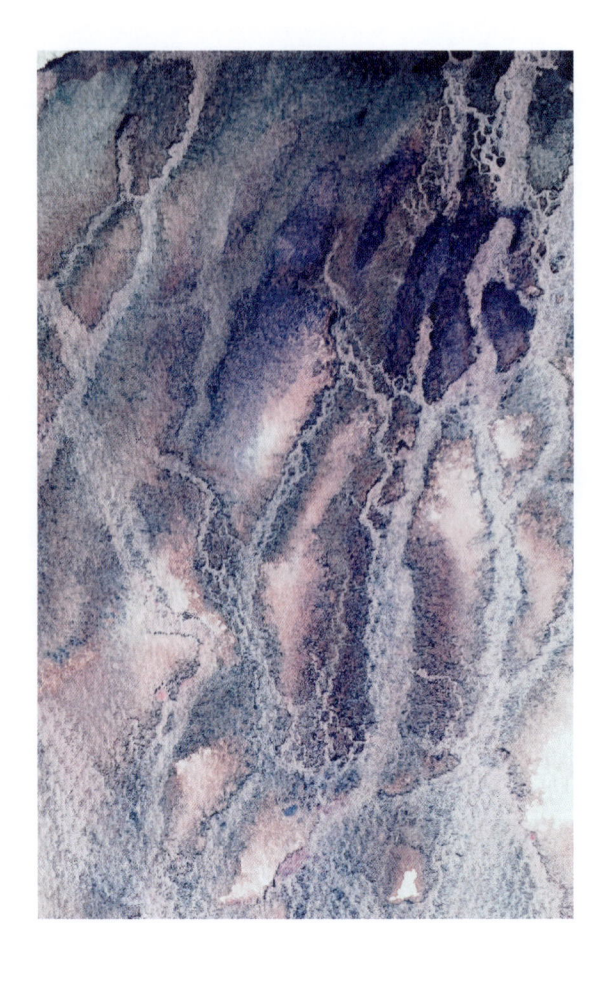

In the stillness

In the stillness of the night, Lord You are there,
A time for reflection and to convey my prayer.

In the stillness of the night, Lord You are there,
As a gentle calmness fills the night time air.

In the stillness of the night, Lord You are there,
As I pray out to You for comfort and care.

In the stillness of the night, Lord all is well.
As I take time to be still and in silence dwell.

In the stillness of the night, Lord You are there,
A time for reflection and to convey my prayer.

Rain and stillness

Rain and stillness

When it's a dark, grey day and the rain seems to keep on falling,
Make time to reflect on the Lord and listen out for His calling.

Reach out to the golden silence and free up your troubled mind,
Embrace the grace and love of the Lord and put all your worries behind.

Such precious moments, solitary and peaceful, full of calmness and ease,
Make time to reflect on the Lord always, especially on rainy days such as these...

Precious stillness

Precious stillness

Life can get so busy, with too many chores to complete,
There never seems enough time, always rushed off one's feet.

Make time to pause and relax in precious silence and peace,
To let all the day's worries fade away and eventually cease.

Make time to seek the presence of the Lord,
in the stillness all around,
To listen out for His voice in the midst of any other sound.

Make time to rest your soul in God alone,
for He hears and He cares,
So, open up your heart to Him and convey your prayers.

Life may always seem busy, yet there is a way,
To feel rested in God's grace and calmness each and every day.

Reflection time/prayer/praise

Reflection time/prayer/praise

Reflection time/prayer/praise